POETRY
&
MILITANCY
IN
LATIN AMERICA

ROQUE DALTON

Azul Editions
2005

Limited Edition Copyright © 2005 Azul Editions
Translation Copyright © 1981 Arlene Scully and
James Scully
All Rights Reserved

This book was originally published as
#1 of the Art on the Line Series,
Curbstone Press, 1981

POETRY AND MILITANCY IN LATIN AMERICA
POESIA Y MILITANCIA EN AMERICA LATINA
appeared originally in CASA DE LAS AMÉRICAS
No. 20-21, September-December, 1963

OLD SHIT
VIEJUEMIERDA
is from *LAS HISTORIAS PROHIBIDAS DEL PULGARCITO*
1974

This limited edition of 100 copies
is published by
Azul Editions
7804 Sycamore Drive
Falls Church, VA 22042

ISBN: 1-885214-29-4

Azul Editions
www.azuleditions.com

POETRY
&
MILITANCY
IN
LATIN AMERICA   7

OLD SHIT   29

AFTERWORD
ON
DALTON'S ESSAY
(JAMES SCULLY)   39

1

What do I propose to do, working in poetry? In general, to express life, that is, the life I witness and help create. My time, its people, the resources we share, along with all their interdependencies. Such is my purpose, starting from the apparently simple fact of being Salvadoran, that is, part of a Latinamerican people which pursues its happiness struggling against imperialism and the creole oligarchy, and which, for quite concrete historical reasons, has a truly impoverished cultural tradition. So impoverished, that only to the slightest extent can it be incorporated in that struggle which has a crying need for every sort of weapon.

These basic facts make every kind of concern consequential by providing my work with a national content, that is, making it expressive of the people of El Salvador. But in speaking of the 'Salvadoran people' I speak of the workers and peasants, of the middle class and, in general, every social sector subject to oligarchic/imperialist oppression — all whose fundamental community interests coincide with the larger interest of building a free, sovereign nation teeming with the best incentives for human progress. That's why, also, I try to write for the people, in a democratic way.

In the preceding general outline of my poetic intentions I have distinguished the needs which, in order to develop my work, I have to set forth and try to satisfy in view of the historic panorama manifesting my people, that is to say, the human medium that grants me roots, a reality to hold onto in time and space. It would be appropriate now to attempt a brief, general appraisal of the personal circumstances under which I engage in creative work. Not out of eagerness to offend modesty, but to provide a rationale for the proposals I will have to make later on.

2

My attitude regarding the ideological content and social consequence of poetic work is basically determined, as I understand it, by two extremes: that of my long and deep bourgeois formative period, and that of the communist militancy I've held to for some years now.

Experience in the ranks of the party has informed my ongoing concern with the problems of the people around me — 'the people' in the fullest sense — and focussed my attention precisely on the fundamental responsibilities one must assume, as well as on the actual ways of carrying out those duties in the course of one's life. But long years in a Jesuit school, my early development in the womb of the meanspirited Salvadoran bourgeoisie, my attachment to irresponsible lifestyles, drawn back in holy terror from sacrifice or from the core problems of the epoch, have left their marks on me. The scars of which, even now, are painful.

This latter fact I've become conscious of, I mean, in keeping with the general self-critical trend we all pursue now, when the people calls for our native sons to be spotless and straightforward. Now then, what I cannot do, in this respect, is cross out the present effects [of the past] with a stroke of the pen. So that — at least for the analysis of my literary potential — it's better to accept that past as a given fact. Surmountable, if one wants, but a given. From a serious analysis of my own poetic work — that which I consider most representative, which best expresses me — I can say that what gets in the way of the viewpoint I now have, as a communist, is the attitude I had before, as a bourgeois: above the intentions of the communist, the consequences of bourgeois roots. In applying these considerations, and questioning how the work of art ought to function in the actual context of El Salvador (and Central America in general) I think it would be well to ask: Has the bourgeois outlook, among us, exhausted all its potential? I personally believe not — and that, furthermore, it is constructive to take advantage of all its creative possibilities, so that we may not only leave its essentially negative aspects behind, but use it as an instrument to create ideal conditions for the new peoples' art that will spring up, no matter what, and reflect the new life that we Salvadorans will know how to win for ourselves. *The possibilities of bourgeois art and culture have not been exhausted* (on the other hand the oligarchy and imperialism have imposed it on the artists, and Salvadorans on the receiving end, in a manner grossly lacking in subtlety) *and so it's well that we revolutionary writers open the way to future art, to the future revolutionary Salvadoran literature, from within the very bowels of bourgeois culture, hastening at the same time its collapse and disintegration by confronting it with its insurmountable internal contradictions, making it face itself and what it springs from — taking it, finally, consciously, with the people's blessed cunning, to the dead end it would come to anyway if we let it develop untroubled in the hands of its logical creators, the bourgeois artists, the artists/ ideologues of the bourgeoisie.*

3

Extending this deliberation, and therefore coming nearer what touches on my own individual work, it would be fitting to pose the following questions: to what extent has the *nation* been manifest in the literature produced thus far in El Salvador? The history of Salvadoran literature . . . is it capable of giving us a vision of the whole of our social development? It would seem not. But if the most significant portion of that literature has been produced in the last fifty or sixty years, that is to say, the lapse of time in which our country has become a semifeudal wasteland dominated by North American imperialism, with a great mass of dispossessed peasantry on one side, a rapacious landed oligarchy on the other, and in the middle a weak, embryonic working class, with an alienated petty bourgeoisie, and the germ of a national bourgeoisie lacking an expansive outlook — can we, in our literature, follow the trail of declarations made by some or each of those classes and ascertain that they are authentic expressions of those classes? Or is it that owing to the economic, political, social and, therefore, cultural distortions that, in our development, the imperialist domination implies — distortion that hinders the classic step-by-step rise of the various social classes into consciousness of themselves *as* classes — it is necessary to propose that all problems of the artistic superstructure correspond to a single, basic, general contradiction, that is, between the people and the nation on one side, and imperialism and its middlemen on the other? Because this being so, all the previous questions could become threadbare, being answerable on the basis of dividing our literature into two parts: that which in general corresponds to, or does not oppose, the interests of the overbearing "two-headed monster" [the creole oligarchy and U.S. imperialism], and that which in general has claimed to be the expression of the people, of their life, their problems, their struggles and hopes. But I suspect the matter is not so simple.

4

Given those two considerations — the needs of Salvadoran literature, and my own personal situation as regards creative work — I became anxious to direct my cultural labor toward the following general objectives that, certainly, I'm still quite far from fulfilling: 1) To fight to have the work of Salvadoran writers and artists of my generation nourish itself on the national reality, the end being to help transform that reality in a revolutionary way. 2) To elucidate, in definitive form, the problem of the Salvadoran cultural tradition so as to incorporate it in our work, along with a new conception of cultural development. That is to say, among other things, to establish its principal constant features, its scope on the universal plane — what is living and what is dead, the useful and the useless — so as to confer on the fragmented Salvadoran culture the essential characteristic of any culture whatever: organic unity, interconnectedness, the grounds of existence at once particularized and whole. And, in keeping with my first general objective: 3) To advocate the scientific understanding of our reality (applying the Marxist-Leninist method) and to back up my creative work with militant activity within the ranks of the Revolution — grand objective of all modern literature or art dedicated to the elevation of humankind.

5

Having made, then, some definitive statements, it is necessary to begin drawing some details and distinctions. I've said that I am a poet who, in relation to political militancy, works within the ranks of the Communist Party. But this fact suggests only that I have social concerns, making clear my direct contact with the organization that, as time will tell, most adequately explains social phenomena. All this generates, in me, a sense of responsibility regarding the human struggle. Further, this responsibility is carried out principally through the specific work of the Party, in concrete acts of the Revolution. My poetry, *besides safeguarding this responsibility with its own particular resources,* pursues other ends, becoming something other than a mere ethical instrument the moment the power of the imagination, among other things, comes into play. Imagination, for instance, heightens reality, and in those circumstances its expression must be, to some extent, more valuable to men, inasmuch as it not only grants them a primary understanding of the real — which could be enough for their fight for liberty — but it puts them in touch with the truly transcendent, we could say eternal, aspects of that reality. Here it may be suitable to call attention to the function, that art and literature have, of 'improving man and nature.' On the other hand there's no need to forget that in pursuing the political end (achievement, on the part of the people, of becoming conscious of itself and of its needs) poetry and art must do so with their own special means, that is to say, artistic means, the most effective as regards *artistically* picking up on the reality that needs to be expressed.

6

For this reason I've been saying for awhile now that the major poet of today must have, to build a body of work, two necessary starting points: profound understanding of life, and his or her own imaginative liberty. So such a poet will have had to live intensely, in the thick of nature and what is human, to have gone down into the dark hollows of his or her heart of hearts, and risen to the glorious dramas of the people, to have borne witness to the nakedness of insects and the catastrophes of orography. Out of this experience, gained through years of hard, wonderful everyday comings and goings, the imagination, with its expressive instruments (style, artistic genre), will be able to undertake the making of the great work of art *if* the proprietor of that imagination has a clear conception of creative freedom and of his or her responsibilities regarding beauty. In the course of this, many helpful material measures may be taken: the incorporation (critical assimilation), in modern creative work, of the cultural tradition of humanity; the satisfactory treatment of myths and the use of the symbol in the sense appropriate to each epoch.

7

Basically the poet must keep faith with poetry, with beauty. He must take the content that his outlook on life and mankind imposes on him (as the great responsibility that goes with coexistence, with living together) and steep it in the abundance of the beautiful. And here there's no room for subterfuges or the inversion of terms. The poet is such because he makes poetry, that is to say, because he creates a beautiful work. While he does something else he will be whatever he wants to be, except a poet. Which certainly does not imply, with respect to the poet, a privileged position among men, but only a precise placement among them and a rigorous limitation of his activity, the same that would also take effect in specifications of the capacities of doctors, carpenters, soldiers and criminals.

8

The poet is communist as well? — I'm asked, more or less. In reply, I'll begin by repeating what I've already said: the great obligation of the poet, communist or not, is to the very essence of poetry, to beauty. This assumes — as professors of algebra are wont to say — the poet's own proper responsibility or, if one prefers, his degree of revolutionary consciousness regarding the concrete demands of the time as they suggest to him — as he carries on with his creative work — the correct thematic trends to follow. And seeing as we're speaking of themes or subjects, I have to add in this area I have an old postulate, one I consider thoroughly honest: all that fits into life fits into poetry. The poet — above all the communist poet — will have to articulate all of life: the proletarian struggle, the beauty of the cathedrals left us by the Spanish Colony, the wonder of the sexual act, the prophecies of the fruitful future that the great signs of the day proclaim to us.

9

Now then, of what beauty do we speak? to what do we refer when we say 'the beautiful?' Clearly we recognize the danger of working with terms that idealism has tried to reclaim for itself. From Plato to the wistful sighing moderns who cling to what was never more than a piece of stupidity, the concept of 'art for art's sake,' some words have been manipulated with such baffling meaning that now it's quite difficult for a revolutionary to use them without being suspected of holding views that mark the opposite philosophic pole. As I've made clear in statements above, when speaking of beauty and the beautiful we don't have to give up for an instant the *grounds* of form. So then, form and content make up an inseparable unity, shaping the artwork. It's in that sense we say beauty is a matter of the very essence of poetry. Moreover we consider the concept of beauty and the beautiful as cultural realities, endowed with historic scope and social roots.

10

And the forms of poetry, of art, that cultivate 'the ugly?' — I'm asked again. This is not a valid argument against the beautiful *essence* of poetry. It is there in the so-called 'ugly' forms, or else the beauty is more hidden than usual (by virtue of the non-traditional means by which it is transmitted) or else it appears by way of contrast.

11

The creative work of the communist poet, I think it's evident, has various levels. Depending on the daily demands of the struggle, the poet immersed in the party of the workers and peasants will have to produce fast-moving agitational slogans, satiric verses, poems that call for the raising of rebellion against oppression. To what extent is the result of this labor poetry? There are unusual cases but in general the result, as regards form, is extremely poor, although in the historical/political field it can become, depending on the circumstances, extremely valuable.

12

The Party must train the poet as a good militant communist, as a valuable cadre for mass revolutionary action. The poet, the artist, must contribute in the utmost to the cultural education of all members of the Party. The Party, specifically, must help the poet develop into an effective agitator, a soldier with expert marksmanship — in a word, a fit cadre. The poet must acquaint all his comrades with Nazim Hikmet or Pablo Neruda, and give them a clear concept of the role of cultural work within the context of general revolutionary activity. He must also make sure that the Administrative Secretary of the Central Committee, for example, loves St. John of the Cross, Henri Michaud, or St. John Perse.

13

It is necessary to root out this false, mechanical, destructive notion whereby the poet committed to his people and his time is an angry or excessively pained individual who goes through life saying, without any further ado, that the bourgeoisie is disgusting, that the most beautiful thing in the world is a union meeting, and that socialism is a garden of yielding roses under an especially mild sun. Life is not so simple, and the sensitivity a Marxist needs to be truly such [*i.e.* Marxist] had better be grasped fully. It is the poet's duty to fight against mechanical, schematic thinking. This schematic approach impedes the development of poetry — which, as conqueror of the cosmos, must keep ever fresh its thirst for adventure — and damages the potentially positive concepts it contains.

14

Someone characterized the poet as one who does not live normally if kept from writing. The structure of that idea is like that of a sentiment which took root in me some years ago: that of the impossibility of doing creative work outside the ranks of the revolution. If the revolution, that is, the struggle of my people, my party, my revolutionary theory, are the pillars on which I wish to base and raise my life, and if I consider life in all its intensity as the great source and substance of poetry, what sense is there in thinking of creation if one abandons the obligations that go with being a man and a militant? Undoubtedly, it makes no sense whatever. And this, it's fitting to explain here, has nothing to do with 'expressive form' nor (if you'll pardon the redundancy) with the response of poetry itself with respect to civil duties.

The sentiment I refer to is solidly backed by genuine objectives. I'll illustrate this point with a few lines from Roger Garaudy, written to summarize conclusions (arrived-at during the 'First Week of Marxist Thought' celebrated in Paris last year) that synthesized and sharply delineated the basic elements that the revolutionary position incorporates in our lives. 'Marxism-Leninism,' says the wise French professor, 'allows us to think and live out the three greatest forces that today move the world as regards the wonderful work of the enlightenment: the most thoroughgoing *humanism*, the most exalted conception of mankind, one with limitless horizons; the most dependable

22

scientific method, that which is inferred from dialectical materialism; and the greatest force for putting this science and this humanism into action — *the proletarian revolution.*' Love of humanity: best means of arriving at the truth, and a force that guarantees hope will be realized. Can one conceive another, better basis for poetry?

15

The revolutionary is, among other things, the person most useful to his epoch. Because he lives to bring about ends that signify the highest interests of humanity. This holds true for the revolutionary poet — as revolutionary and as poet — in that, from the publication of his first word he is addressing all people in defense of their own highest longings. Therefore it's foolish to so much as even discuss the matter with those who assert that, in poetry, the social function and the humanist posture are, at the least, extrapoetic elements. Foolish, mainly, because such discussion of itself implies a renunciation, *a priori*, of the universality of poetry.

16

It is a fine thing to think of the poet as a prophet. In itself such regard is a poetic act in that the creator of poems seems to look out, from the forested heights, over the future of humanity, and to point out the great pathways. I prefer, however, to pinpoint the poet more as a scrutinizer of his own time than of the future, because, like it or not, by insisting too much on what will come we lose at some level our immediate perspective, and we run the risk of not being understood by all the people who find themselves immersed in everyday life. The very problem of Revolution deserves to be approached — within the poetic undertaking — from this point of view. A case in point: should we revolutionary Latinamerican poets concentrate our labor on the foretelling of socialist society before raising, to the category of poetic material, the contradictions, disasters, defects, customs and struggles of our present society? I sincerely believe not. I consider that the average reader in the capitalist world, in order to be convinced of the necessity for Revolution, will have to know, among other things, how the crude intellectual schemes of the bourgeoisie are structured, plus the sordidness of individual deeds in their capitalist subworld, and the clash between noble humanistic sentiments and the ambiance that comes of exploitation. Besides, I realize that the reader must be given the opportunity to become acquainted with new points of view about life, events and people, for instance about the nation's history, which has had an expurgated version imposed on it by the ruling class — a distortion that literature, through its own specific resources, would have very little difficulty in combatting. Only after such labor, involving (I don't pass over it) a great deal of destructive activity, is it possible to begin constructing, without major obstacles, the prospectus of the future. And it is necessary to call attention to one essential aspect of this viewpoint: I hold this thesis to be valid in the preparatory stage, the insurrectional stage and in the triumphal stage of any Latimamerican revolution. Including when that revolution is already on the road toward the construction of socialism. Although in this latter case, obviously, it would continue only partly in effect.

17

Honor of the revolutionary poet: to convince his or her generation of the necessity for being revolutionary here and now, in the difficult period, the only one that has the potential to be subject of an epic. To be revolutionary when the revolution has eliminated its enemies and has in every sense consolidated itself can be, no doubt about it, more or less glorious and heroic. But to be so when the condition of being revolutionary is usually rewarded with death, that is truly the dignity of poetry. The poet takes then the poetry of his or her generation and gives it over to history.

OLD SHIT

There was, in El Salvador, a teacher and journalist
named don Alberto Masferrer.

He was born in the little town of Alegría,
        District of Usulután,
and dedicated himself to denouncing social injustices
in books, such as *Curséd Money* and *Letters to a Worker*,
and editorials in a newspaper he founded, called
        Fatherland.

In this poem we shall try to explain
some of the reasons why such a man
has been canonized and institutionalized
as a national philosopher/sociologist/prophet
by the line of dictatorships the country has endured,
a fact that has left some simple souls wondering.

Said simple souls ask, why get so worked up over
this man called 'a wing against the hurricane,'
'the dread Salvadoran St. John,' 'the great
crusher of lies,' 'the awesome
agitator of the country,' particularly
in a country as essentially unjust
as is El Salvador.

His story is not uncommon in the tropics.

Caught in the cultural currents
of a muddled turn-of-the-century Latin America,
don Alberto walked forever on the wave of
        Domingo Faustino Sarmiento
in that, all the while, he mistook the poor for savages,
he absorbed the global anguish of the bourgeoisie
        which produces reformism
and got stoned to the eyeballs with mysterious oriental
        philosophies.
He fell in love with words, words alone,
and believed in, and meticulously underwrote
the rigmarole of 'tongue lashing,' the
whopper mask of fat scoundrels like
        Monsignor Castro Ramírez,
the machete of all the congressmen of the Official Party,
the best relief valve for the pressure cooker in which
we all live, fit to burst, from sunrise to sunset.

He wanted to be like Gandhi, but lacked
        profundity, history,
actual confrontation with the main enemy of his country.
He dreamed of becoming like José Ingenieros
but lacked the talent, the information, the courage to
        hold firmly in his hands
the classic texts of Marxism.
He turned into a sort of Gabriela Mistral who didn't write
        poetry.
From Christianity he learned the patience
        of the other cheek.
And against violence he raised the lettuce head of
        vegetarianism.

He preached chastity, anti-alcoholism and literacy,
man's right to clean air and water,
to sufficient, varied, nutritious and wholesome food,
    and well-ventilated,
to Justice (with a capital J) that is quick, easy, equally
    accessible to all,
and to a primary education effectively rounded out
forming hearty men, skilled workers and heedful
    heads of families.

But he was quite guarded about explaining how those
    wonders
might be secured, in a way fair to everyone.
The most he did was refer us
to the responsibility of Government and to the majesty of
    Law,
to the Will of God and the good graces of the rich,
to self improvement through infinite patience
and to the fruits of general education and universal
    culture.

At first nearly everyone died laughing
at the impotent rage of four or so baldheads, his
    disciples.
Later, those who died laughing most at the oafishness of
    don Alberto,
assured that his diatribes did little more than tickle them,
began to figure out how all that thought
could be useful to them.
Above all, faced with other thoughts that went around
    raising a ruckus among the people

with words that proposed going beyond words
and that, in short, recommended the machetes of the
>>poor
not be left stuck in their sheathes

but let us continue with the doctrine of don Alberto

who had his picture perfect politics
picture perfect:
he left word that the drive to attain
all that was termed 'the vital minimum'
ought to derive from men committed to the New Faith
who moreover accepted, as personal commandments,
>>precepts
to be diligent workers,
to help their children and parents (who were always
>>old and needy),
to contribute to the upkeep of orphanages, hospitals
and poorhouses in their commune or province;
to protect harmless animals, especially the birds;
to respect and protect trees;
to be cleancut and well-spoken;
not to get drunk or drugged up;
not to risk gambling away the fruits of labor, nor dissipate
>>nor prostitute oneself;
to cultivate no vice, nor live by usury, nor by
>>expropriating someone else's work;
to watch over the rights of children
and not allow oneself, neither for pay nor because
>>of threats,
to serve as the tool of any tyranny.

If Utopia is the codification
of the greatest number of human aspirations
without enclosing a specific, effective method
for their realization,
don Alberto Masferrer was a typical utopian
but of a low order, underdeveloped, wanting
imaginative power.

But isn't it perhaps asking too much of don Alberto
— who was, after all, a Full Professor misplaced in El Salvador
at the beginning of the century —
this demanding of him a methodology,
a policy, tactics
from his ubiquitous pulpit? Is it perhaps
that he did not make, and then some, a first-rate job of it
in pointing out many of our social ills?

Perhaps, among us, pointing out evil is not yet
to denounce it, the first
step toward rising up against it?

Don Alberto, if we're to have him an honest man
(though the problem, in this mess, is not honesty)
apparently truly believed it was.

What's more, he believed it to the point of granting verbal
denunciation
so much autonomy
that, for him, 'the burning word' became the only reality,
independent, deep down, of the real reality that
gave it birth.
But even in this belief he contradicted himself

for soon he realized that in El Salvador merely
speaking can bring down, on one, all kinds of trouble.

Longing for the audience an intellectual has in
                cultured circles
don Beto reproached us with the facts that
"Tolstoy was heard in the land of the Czars, without
                anyone trying
to skin him alive," and that
"if they imprisoned Eliseo Reclus
it wasn't for his ideas, but because he took part in
                the Commune."

That is to say, in essence:
"Persuasive words alone are not enough
except as substitutes for action.
And when our persuasive words are met with threats
why then, we must elevate our rhetoric."

That is what don Alberto thought
and thus he came to acquire fame as a prophet.
(Whether there, deep in his heart,
he was a good person or not, is another kettle of fish,
fish that never filled anyone's belly.)

Besides, in this misty world
even 'the burning word' goes to rot:
that of Masferrer rotted in the lifetime of him
                who uttered it
and rotted in its law, in its own forms of being
                and being used.

Let's look at an example.

"Note well," says don Beto, as his first premise in
        Reading and Writing,
"we are not yet a nation."

"Because this country," he adds then, his expression
        growing more profound,
"as it is presently constituted, is a monster."
To read this is an intellectual hair-raiser.
What a lucid man! one thinks, to have written this
        before '32!

But then, in *Culture Through Books,* don Alberto gives
        his reasoning:
"It is evident that a third of our 48 cities," he says,
"(more or less 48) do not have
as cultural apparatuses
(aside from the church and town hall, which are
        ramshackle and cobwebby)
more than a barnyard and a state-run tobacco shop.
        Worse yet
many of those cities have neither water
nor toilets in their houses."

And he ends up shouting (the 'dread St. John'):
"How could they possibly permit the construction of
a house without a toilet?
How could they possibly dignify, with the title 'city,'
a handful of barbarians
who still do not feel the need for toilets!?"

Such is the word dodge:
to denounce the infinite generality of evil
while proposing solutions the size of an ant.

The present social system is unjust? we dig latrines.
Burglaries overwhelm us? we leave, as pawns, old
              clothing in the backyard
so the good thief won't have to go any farther.
Prostitution proliferates? we teach the girls to read.
Exploitation is the principal human relationship
              throughout the country? we pray.

It's not simply a matter of preferring words over actions:
it's a matter of setting up words
that with their glitter
or the glitter of fantastic solutions
blot out the profound resonance of reality, its
              fundamental truth.

This is one of the booby traps
he set us up on, that old shithead,
suction pump of idiocy that today politicians
and colonels
and the most contriving, baldfaced professors
and venerable leaders of youth with their sweaty hands
and Ad Agencies
and political parties that regard themselves as nationalist
              and democratic
and bishops who carry on as liberals
and professionals disguised as decent deodorized folk
and the roving ears of the CIA
who establish garden clubs or

Centralamericanism
and the owners of Major Press and Television
and Ministers of Education with their
               editorial departments
and the homosexual cults of Foreign Relations
spew forth into the spiritual depths of our youth
to squelch their rebellion,
to liquidate their wonderful impulses through the
               God Boob Tube,
their blessed rage through the God Drug.

And this, without denying don Beto could have written
               everything with the best intentions.
Because if we had proof that all the harm he did the
               country
was, from the word go, intentional,
we'd be obliged to go dig him up
and bring his bones over to the cranny where General
               Martínez rots away
along with don Foncho Quiñónez Molina, and
               the Meléndezes.

A mishmash of con man, holy idiot, and exasperated
               great grandaddy
don Beto was, however, in his lifetime
even accused of being communist.
And, for the crowning blow,
after the 1932 massacre he himself believed it
and went off to die of melancholy in Guatemala,
believing himself to blame for having misled
               so many to death.

Nor did he realize he would pass into our cultural history
(when the true history of our culture is written)
as an objective accomplice of the people's assassins,
those he had offered a more refined, disarming means
for exploitation and domination.

Don Beto Masferrer serves, today, all purposes.

Consolation for wives of drunks,
wheatfield picked over by hacks who write the
                President's speeches,
elephant graveyard
where leftist intellectuals tired of life
arrive with their briefcase ideology
and set it down by the pillow to die once and for all
thinking how nice it might have been, in life and ever
                after,
if the struggle had not been so hard
in the dwarf country that finally got to one.

AFTERWORD ON DALTON'S ESSAY (JAMES SCULLY)

Roque Dalton: wry, witty. Caustic. A militant communist poet whose irony penetrates, as in the sidewinding epigram on "General Martínez:"

> They say he was a good President
> because he allotted cheap housing
> to the Salvadorans who were left . . . *

Yet "Poetry and Militancy in Latin America" has little of the irony or the razory singlemindedness of Dalton's poetry. He does persist in awkward, excoriating honesty: true to the world as is, to himself, and to the relationship between them. But he is not inclined to mock, nor even to be companionable with that bittersweet charm of his. The voice is tentative, unassured, going from back-off academic all the way over to heroic, fleetingly romantic deliveries. So the reader may suspect the essay communicates more than it says. And it does. It is as much drama as essay, a symptom as well as a saying.

Surrounding and conditioning this are intimations of a complex, unresolved life — the life of a principled yet realistic man who no longer even dreams of an easy way out. What are the circumstances? Where and when was this published? For whom written? By whom?

---

*Martínez, who ruled from 1932 to 1944, had taken power by killing 4,000 rebels (who had risen in response to overturned elections) and organizing, within weeks, the massacre of 30,000 peasants, Indians, trade unionists and members of the Salvadoran Communist Party — 4% of the entire population.

In 1963 Dalton was 30 years old, had escaped imprisonment in El Salvador, and was living in exile. The essay, as most of his poetry, was published in Cuba. It must be read in terms of its audience. Or audiences. Dalton had more than one in mind, though not at the same time.

Some are Cuban fellow artists — like him, communists and party members, but unlike him in being over the threshold of a developing revolution and in a relatively safe, 'socialist' environment. Dalton himself must contend with disadvantages that this audience has no experience of. He must work in exile or survive in El Salvador under the threat of imprisonment, torture and death. Still other problems are historical in a different sense: for instance, his effort to express a country that has not yet entered into a phase even of *bourgeois* nationalism. And some disadvantages appear as advantages, such as his having been raised in privilege, amidst spectacular exploitation and poverty, and formed throughout his youth by Jesuit schooling (manifest perhaps in the intellectual impatience and acerbic militancy of much of his poetry).

He also speaks, or talks back, to the more superficial and brittle verities of the Communist Party leadership. And he becomes, by turns, patient, indirect, teacherly, defensive, aggressive, ambivalent. Aside from himself (the internal dialogue and struggle are pervasive) this seems to be the audience that he is most acutely, and uneasily, conscious of.

Here the issues he raises are especially instructive. For one, the insistence on creative freedom — on not only allowing the *committed* poet his or her initiative (the qualification, though implicit, is definitely present), but permitting the inclusion of all aspects of life, not just approved ones. The latter demand, of course, could be put to any establishment of academicism, whatever its ostensible politics.

Also he observes, almost in passing, that slogans and agitational verses are called-for on occasion, and that they may be truly useful, though seldom achieving the status of art.* Given stereotypical views of the 'Party writer' as a hack who must produce slogans, one might expect Dalton to dwell on this matter. His cursory treatment suggests that the problem, if there is one, is neither recurrent nor exceptionally intense.

The pressing issues are much subtler. For example: the injunction to describe the world dialectically, in terms of what it is becoming, and thus to present history constructively, in terms of a developing working class and its eventual triumph through socialism. The responsibility (for that is what it is) to see and understand the

---

*It should be noted that, contrary to scholastic belief, slogans are not inherently inferior or simplistic. They demand extraordinary decisiveness, concreteness and lucidity. Most of all they demand realization. Their power is in the potential for crystallizing and mobilizing communities. The main difficulty, aside from the stresses of more or less collective creation, is that slogans cannot survive flaws. They stand exposed, unhedged, subject to open challenge from the reality they would confront and transform (the reality that *all* literature, whatever the form, must ultimately measure up to).

world in such a manner is based on profound respect for the dynamic nature of reality. But when this responsibility is accepted and projected in a mechanical way, it degenerates into just another instance of idealist thought whereby there is no 'becoming,' only the 'being' that is and the 'being' that is to come. (Such 'being,' with its false implication of stasis, and its mystification of process mechanisms, is no more than a 'seeming,' an illusion.) This is the tendency that Dalton takes seriously, and takes pains to reject, particularly as it is used to push ahistorical abstractions. For him, the poet must deal with the present *as is*, rather than try to overleap it or to project a future, an audience and a language that have not as yet been historically realized.*
Here, anyway, he invokes a historical materialist consideration — over against the cynicism and despair of a merely assertive utopianism. He is too sincere, too practical, to imagine a goal without also imagining, and trying out, the steps by which it might be arrived-at.

So he turns to his Salvadoran compatriots. These he exhorts: to teach them and win them over. His intent is to promote a socialist, or rather a modified 'anti-imperialist,' national culture. Which is also why he, much like Cardenal in Nicaragua, writes so much historical verse — both of them formulating and bringing to light the suppressed histories of their respective, in fact overlapping, territories.

---

*Of course the corrective has its own pitfalls. As Engels noted, responding to the editor of a proposed multi-volume anthology of revolutionary poetry, "In general, the poetry of past revolutions (the *Marseillaise* always excepted) rarely has a revolutionary effect for later times because it must also reproduce the mass prejudices of the period in order to affect the masses. Hence the religious nonsense even among the Chartists . . ." [letter to Hermann Schüter, 15 May 1885]

Yet, as often happens, the anti-imperialist outlook gives way to nationalism, in effect resolving into a non-class analysis in which 'socialism' is retained as a sentiment, a conscience, but abandoned as a guide to ongoing practice. Dalton's phrase, 'my people,' is not synonymous with 'workers of all countries,' but is at once less focused regarding class commitment (qualitative deterioration) and more exclusive (quantitative decline). Certainly this shift did not make him any less militant. In what he did as in what he wrote, Dalton remained a fighter. But the resulting political incoherence left his poetry, sharp and impressive as it is, somewhat at a loss. It forced him ever more deeply into the bind of an ironic attitude.

He is seldom ironic here, however, not even when responding to bourgeois assumptions, usually in order to dismiss them. Their perspective being almost entirely the reflection of an ideological warp, he does not take them seriously. The one exception occurs where he partly gives in to their assumptions, and partly reacts against the flat, self-mutilating utilitarianism of his more abstracted comrades, by asserting the need for 'beauty.' Doubtless the notion of beauty has been so abused that it needs defending. Yet even if we think we know what he means, and if we sympathize with his intent, still his claim is unconvincing because it begs the question. He does what too many others (including Marxists) have done in presuming, without analysis, the necessity for an unspecified 'artistic quality,' as though 'beauty' or 'artistic quality' were self-born, self-sufficient essences rather than classbound, materially conditioned terms. Naturally he distinguishes his own use of this concept — intimating that it is historical, not metaphysical — from that of the 'art for art's sake' fantasizers of virginbirths. But the blur remains.

What is more interesting is his avowed aim of using bourgeois culture against itself in order to hasten the exhaustion of that culture's resources and, thereby, to move beyond it. In part this is a rationalization for his own reliance on critical irony. But it also stands opposed to the radical notion of destroying bourgeois culture completely, so as to start afresh.* Then again it does not coincide with, though more closely resembling, Lenin's position, which was to overcome cultural backwardness by incorporating and using the techniques and traditions of past culture.**

---

*Historically associated with some 'Left' artists in the early years of the Bolshevik Revolution; with the Proletkult, most acutely in its later stages; and with the Cultural Revolution in China.

**See Lenin's intervention in the 1920 Proletkult Congress, as he attempts to head off not only their claim to organizational autonomy, but their move to throw out all of bourgeois culture: "Marxism has won its historic significance as the ideology of the revolutionary proletariat because, far from rejecting the most valuable achievements of the bourgeois epoch, it has, on the contrary, assimilated and refashioned everything of value in the more than two thousand years of the development of human thought and culture. Only further work on this basis and in this direction, inspired by the practical experience of the proletarian dictatorship as the final stage in the struggle against every form of exploitation, can be recognized as the development of a genuine proletarian culture." [On Proletarian Culture, 8 October 1920]

Curiously, especially in light of the aborted Cultural Revolution a quarter of a century later, Mao at Yenan held a similar view: "We should take over the rich legacy and the good traditions in literature and art that have been handed down from past ages in China and foreign countries, but the aim must still be to serve the masses of the people. Nor do we refuse to utilize the literary and artistic forms of the past, but in our hands these old forms, remoulded and infused with new content, also become something revolutionary in the service of the people." [Talks at the Yenan Forum; conclusion 23 May 1942]